Thud, thud, thud

My big brother's got some new trainers.
He wears them all the time.

Thud, thud, thud! When he runs upstairs
in them the whole house shakes.

Mum shouts, 'Stop that noise!'

My brother's new trainers are big and
puffy and purple. They've got soles as
thick as tractor tyres.

Clump, clump. He's clumping to his
bedroom.

'Gangway!' he shouts.

I have to squash myself against the
wall. So my feet don't get crushed.

'I hate your horrible trainers!' I tell him.
'They're dangerous.'

But he just clumps downstairs again.
Thud, thud, thud. The front door slams.

Thank goodness – he's gone out.

It's nice and peaceful now. I can lie here on the floor and read my book.

Stomp, stomp, stomp.

The floor begins to tremble.

Is a herd of elephants heading this way?

No, it's the new trainers. Here they come again – like great, purple, crushing machines.

'Mind my book. You're trampling on it!'

My big brother throws himself into a chair. He props his big purple feet up on one another.

'I can't see the telly now! It's my favourite programme. Your trainers are in the way!'

Mum says: 'Those new trainers are a menace! Take them off in the house!'

But my brother says, 'I love my new trainers. They're great! I'm never going to take them off! Not ever!'

'Then do up those dangly laces!' sighs Mum. 'You'll break your neck!'

But my brother just clumps outside. His long laces dangle behind him. And his monster trainers squash all the little daisies on the grass.

I hate those new trainers. They should be banned.

My brother even wants to go to bed in his new trainers.

But Mum says: 'I've never heard of anything so silly! Take them off!'

So he climbs up to his top bunk bed. He throws down his new trainers, *whump, whump*, so they land near my bottom bunk bed.

Mum switches off our light.

I lie in the dark and watch the dangerous trainers.

They seem to be even bigger at night. They've got two big purple tongues that stick out at me and go, 'Ya boo!' They've got lots of little eyes, like a spider.

The eyes are watching me back! The trainers are alive!

'Don't be so silly,' I tell myself. 'Trainers can't be alive.'

I close my eyes so I can't see the trainers any more. Then I fall asleep.

But next morning, when I wake up, the trainers have moved! There's no doubt about it.

They're under my brother's computer desk now. And they're neatly side by side.

My big brother didn't move them because he's still in the top bunk, snoring.

'You've been out, haven't you?' I wag my finger at the trainers. 'When we were all asleep you went out on your own, didn't you?'

But the trainers don't say a word.

'Wait until tonight,' I warn them.
'I didn't see you go out last night because
I fell asleep. But tonight I'll stay awake. I'll
catch you, just wait and see.'

The top bunk's creaking. My big
brother's waking up.

A life of their own

'Your trainers are alive,' I tell him. 'They
go out at night on their own, without you.
You know those little metal holes where
you put the laces? Well, they aren't lace
holes. They're eyes. Your trainers have got
lots of eyes, like spiders. Did you know
that? And they've got big slurpy purple
tongues.'

But my brother just groans, 'You do talk a load of rubbish!' Then he turns over and goes back to sleep.

Those trainers are getting me really mad. They're wrecking my things. Today I found my crayons mashed into the carpet.

'You shouldn't have left them on the floor,' said my brother.

But I bet those trainers did it.

Clump, clump, clump. You can't get away from them. You can hear them all over the house.

'Who squashed this chewing gum into the carpet?' shouts Mum.

'It's these trainers,' says my big brother. 'I haven't got used to them yet. They're so big and heavy I can't control them. They keep treading on things!'

'Don't be silly,' says Mum. 'It's your fault, not your trainers. You're talking as if your trainers have a life of their own.'

Mum doesn't know it. But she's exactly right. Those trainers do have a life of their own. They have a secret life. They go out at night, on their own, when we're all asleep. They must do, mustn't they? How else could they be in a different place by morning?

Tonight I'm going to prove it. I'm going to follow those trainers and see where they go. I'm going to spy on them.

It's night time. It must be very late because the house is quiet. Mum and Dad are in bed. But I'm not asleep. I'm watching those trainers, like I said I would.

It's hard work. My eyes keep closing.

'Don't fall asleep!' I whisper to myself. 'Stay awake!'

The trainers are behaving themselves so far. They haven't moved at all. But their spider eyes are glittering in the dark.

I don't trust them. They're very sneaky. As soon as I close my eyes they'll be off, on their own.

But my eyelids are *so* heavy. My head is dropping down. ZZZZZZZZZZZZZZZ –

The trainers are on the move! I knew it!
I knew they had a secret life.

They're marching down the stairs.
Clump, clump, clump. What if they wake up
Mum and Dad? But they don't. Even
though they're making an awful din.

I slip out of bed and follow them. I tip-
toe down the stairs in my bare feet.

At the bottom of the stairs the trainers stop. They look around.

'Ah ha,' I think. 'You're trapped now. The front door is locked.'

But the trainers aren't trapped. Have you ever seen a hamster squeeze through a tiny space? The trainers can do that. They squeeze, like purple toothpaste, through the letter box. First one, then the other.

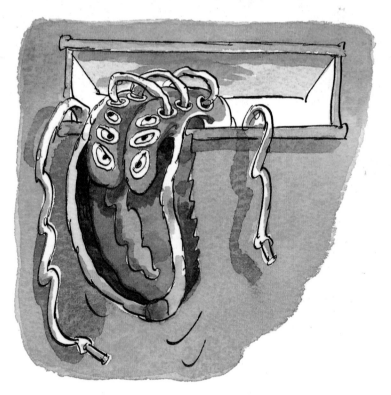

Oh no, they're escaping. I look out
through the glass bit in the front door.
They're stomping down the garden path!

I turn the key in the front door and let
myself out. Mum would go mad if she
knew. It's very late. There's a big silver
moon in the sky. And I'm out here in the
garden, in my pyjamas.

But I'm on a mission. I'm finding out all about the secret life of trainers. I'm finding out what they do when we're all asleep.

I hide behind a bush and spy on them.

At first, they look very innocent.

They're walking round the garden in the moonlight. Just walking.

'That's not dangerous,' I think. 'They're just out for a walk, that's all. A walk in the moonlight.'

But no.

A moth flies by.

And suddenly, the trainers spring into action. One of them throws out a lace like a lasso.

Got it! The moth flutters. But it can't get free. Then the big purple tongue flicks out and, *gulp*, the moth is gone.

I can't believe it! The trainers aren't taking a walk. They're hunting. Hunting for things to eat. My brother's trainers are carnivorous!

They're very good hunters. They guzzle everything in sight.

A shiny black beetle trundles across the grass. He doesn't stand a chance. *Flick* goes the lace and he's dragged into the trainer's purple throat. *Crunch, crunch.*

'*Burp!*' goes the trainer.

A worm pops its head up. *Wham!* goes a trainer and stomps on it. The other trainer licks it up with its tongue.

The trainers sniff the air. They're looking for something else to gobble.

I hear a rustling in the bushes. A baby mouse pops out its pink nose. Oh no!

The trainers' eyes gleam at each other. They stay very, very quiet. They're waiting.

The baby mouse darts out of the grass.

'Run, mouse, run!' I shout. 'You're in deadly danger. The trainers will gobble you up! Run for your life!'

Leave them alone!

But the baby mouse doesn't hear me. He doesn't know what danger he's in. He doesn't know about carnivorous trainers.

He pitter-patters nearer, nearer. Fast as you can blink, the laces flick out. He's tied up like an Egyptian mummy! A big purple tongue slides out and –

'Will you stop shouting?' says my brother. 'I'm trying to get some sleep!'

I sit up in bed. 'I saw them. I saw your trainers. They were out in the garden hunting! They crunch beetles. They lick up worms. They tied a baby mouse up like a mummy!'

'What?' says my brother, rubbing his eyes. 'Did you say a baby mouse?'

'Yes!' I cry. 'And I can prove it! Look, they're not where you left them, are they? They're in a different place!'

My brother looks down from the top bunk bed. The trainers aren't where he threw them. They're neatly side by side, next to the book case.

Mum switches on the light. 'What's the matter? Who was shouting?'

'He was,' says my brother, pointing at me. 'He's being silly, as usual. He says he saw my trainers try to eat a baby mouse. He says they've been out in our garden hunting!'

'Well, why have they moved over there?' I shout at him. 'They weren't there when we went to sleep. That proves they've been out somewhere!'

'Oh, that,' says Mum. 'I moved them. I always come in when you're asleep and tidy up a bit. Haven't you noticed how this bedroom's always neat and tidy when you wake up?'

'No,' says my brother.

'But I saw them,' I tell Mum. 'I saw them out in the garden just now. They were munching a moth!'

'You just had a bad dream,' says Mum.
'That's all.'

And she switches off the light.

'Are you still awake?' I ask my brother,
in the dark.

'Yes,' comes a voice from the top bunk.

'I did see them,' I tell him. 'Honestly, it
wasn't a dream. I should watch out if I
were you. I wouldn't put my feet in those
trainers. Not for a million pounds. They
might nibble your toes. They might gobble
your feet!'

'Just go to sleep,' says my brother.

But he sounds a bit worried.

The next day the house is very quiet.
No *thud, thud.* No *clump, clump.* I can walk
around in my bare feet. I can lie on the
floor and read my book.

Where are the big, purple, mouse-
guzzling trainers?

'I left them on the bus,' says my brother.

Mum goes mad. 'They were brand-new trainers. They cost a lot of money!'

'Sorry,' says my brother. 'It was an accident. Honest it was.'

Mum phones the bus company. Nobody's seen a pair of big, puffy, purple trainers with soles like tractor tyres.

'I can't understand it,' says Mum. 'There's no sign of them. They can't have walked off the bus by themselves!'

My brother and I look at each other. But we daren't grin because Mum's in a bad mood.

Keep your eyes open. One of these days, *you* might see a pair of big purple trainers. You might see them in the moonlight, clumping round your garden. You might hear a tiny '*Squeak, squeak!*' Then a '*Burp!*'

I'd leave them alone if I were you. I'd keep right out of their way.

And I wouldn't put my feet in them. Not even one little pink toe. Putting your toes inside a pair of carnivorous trainers could be very, very dangerous.

About the author

Before I started writing stories for children, I was
a teacher for ten years.

I have three children of my own. They give me
lots of ideas for stories. Here's
how I got the idea for this
story. One day my big son,
Alex, bought a new pair of
shoes. They were enormous!
When he clumped around in
them the whole house
shook. Things got crushed
beneath them – crayons,
books, fingers, toes. My little son, Christopher,
said 'Those are dangerous trainers!' And I thought,
'Dangerous Trainers? That's a good title for a story...'

Other Treetops books at Stages 10 and 11 include:

Purple Buttons by Angela Bull
The Great Spaghetti Suit by Alan MacDonald
Janey's Giants by Nick Warburton
Hilda's Big Chance by John Coldwell
An Odd Job for Bob and Benny by Nick Warburton

Also available in packs
Stage 10/11 pack B   0 19 916902 0
Stage 10/11 class pack B   0 19 916903 9